© 2018 HEIDI J. ELLSWORTH AND KAREN L. EDWARDS

Table of Contents

INTRODUCTION - WHY DO I NEED A MARKETING PLAN? 5

CHAPTER 1 - STRUCTURE OF A MARKETING PLAN 9

CHAPTER 2 - COMPANY POSITIONING STATEMENT 15

CHAPTER 3 - UNDERSTANDING YOUR MARKET 21

CHAPTER 4 - YEARLY GOALS AND INITIATIVES 27

CHAPTER 5 - BRANDING..33

CHAPTER 6 -MARKETING TOOLS AND INITIATIVES..................................43

CHAPTER 7 - TECHNOLOGY CONSIDERATIONS 55

CHAPTER 8 - BUDGETING..65

CHAPTER 9 - TASKS AND TIMELINE 71

CHAPTER 10 - EXECUTIVE SUMMARY...75

CHAPTER 11- IMPLEMENTING & COMMUNICATING THE PLAN.................79

APPENDIX 1 –MARKETING PLAN STRUCTURE 84

APPENDIX 2 – TARGET MARKETS..85

APPENDIX 3 – SAMPLE MARKETING PLANNER 86

APPENDIX 4 - MARKETING BUDGET TEMPLATE.......................................87

CONCLUSION...88

Introduction - Why do I need a marketing plan?

You may be asking yourself, "Why do I need a marketing plan?" It is a good question. A marketing plan is part of your overall business plan. In fact, that marketing plan should be developed after your company's business plan. Marketing is an integral part of business success and can help define and refine the company's goals.

Marketing for roofing contractors can be confusing, frustrating and elusive. Most roofing contractors are craftsmen and women who have started businesses by understanding and excelling at roofing, waterproofing and building envelope technology. They are not marketing professionals, so it is hard to change gears and figure out how to sell or promote their services while also running operations, estimating, sales and the business overall. A good marketing plan helps drive marketing without having to worry all the time.

By taking the time up front to strategize and plan on how to market your business successfully, it enables you to move on to other challenges of the day, week or month. A good plan can be the template for what needs to happen daily, weekly and monthly to keep marketing on task. It also eliminates daily questions or sales calls for additional marketing initiatives. By creating and sticking to a yearly plan, you are simplifying the day-to-day decisions that can stymie progress.

Fewer approvals and more action reduces the stress put on decision makers and puts the action into the hands of the marketing professionals. Whether it is a person in the office, an agency or a marketing coordinator implementing the marketing plan, by being prepared ahead of time you will reduce the stress of making reactive decisions or worse, doing nothing due to lack of time and/or planning.

A good marketing plan will also save you money. As we noted, without a plan it is easy to say yes to that advertising sales person from the local media or free coupon website; or that great new advertising concept for ad words or events that is purchased mid-year without planning or research. It can cost the company in lost time, low productivity and extra expense when you do not budget in advance. By having a preset plan and budget, you can still move money around if necessary but there is a set allocation to work within.

Timing is important. Look at starting your yearly marketing plan in the Fall. It should be a planned exercise to review the past year and look at the upcoming year. Reviewing statistics, campaigns and lead/close ratio is important before starting on the tactical plans for advertising, PR and direct marketing. By organizing budgeting meetings or even off-site working retreats with your leadership team (ideally comprised of leadership from sales, operations, accounting and marketing), you can take the time to review past goal performance or obtainment while setting new goals that reflect growth. By being conscious of past performance, you will set the stage for developing strong marketing programs for the next year.

In fact, you should not even start looking at a marketing plan until you have your goals set. What are the company's plans for growth next year? Will there be new services or products? Will there be any changes in overall company mission? Marketing supports the goals of the company and supports the sales team in obtaining the revenue and profitability goals that make a company successful. If you do not have strong goals and plans, then marketing will most likely flounder.

Regarding sales, it is critical that marketing works hand-in-hand with sales. The marketing plan needs to reflect the goals of the sales team so that the marketing activities are nurturing and delivering the right leads for sales success. If the goal is to grow metal roofing but marketing is delivering asphalt shingle leads that are not upgradable, both teams will fail.

By understanding the type of customers, the sales team is looking for and the products and services they will be selling, a marketing plan can be created that will result in success for all departments as well as for the company.

As the plan is being developed, also remember to keep an eye on your competition and industry trends. By taking the time to understand the competition's marketing strategies, you can differentiate your company to be more appealing; and be the first to close the sale. By being involved in the larger industry through trade associations and media outlets, you will find ideas that may be working in other parts of the country but have not been tried in your region. It is not about creating all the ideas but about implementing the right ideas for your customers and market.

By creating a marketing plan for your roofing business, you are taking the time to determine the ideal customer for your business and how you will attract, convert, close and delight that customer. A good marketing plan that is well thought out will address every stage of the sales and marketing process and detail how you will retain the attention of past customers while also gaining ongoing referrals.

The last reason why you need a marketing plan is communication. By taking the time to review, strategize and commit to paper your marketing plans, you are providing a communication vehicle for your company all year long. It should be shared with all employees, so they understand the goals of the sales and marketing teams and can help support them in the office and the field. By including the company in your plans for growth and marketing, your employees will help you as your brand ambassadors, sharing the correct message to customers and strangers alike.

So, let's get started. Every chapter will have action items. As with our first book, *Sales and Marketing for Roofing Contractors*, we recommend that you gather your leadership team and use this as a guide and workbook for creating a marketing plan. It does not need to happen all at once. A chapter a week with discussion, homework and task assignments will help lead your team into a good planning meeting ending with a strong working marketing plan for the new year or for whenever you start.

CHAPTER 1

Structure of a Marketing Plan

Now that you have decided to put a marketing plan together, you need to understand what should be included in the plan. This chapter will review the different sections that make up the plan, including the executive summary, company position, markets, yearly goals and initiatives, branding, marketing tools, tasks, timelines, budget and implementation. Following chapters will follow the structure of a marketing plan and help you work through each section specifically for your company. The goal is for you to have a working marketing plan at the end of this book.

Executive summary
Your completed plan will open with an executive summary that is written after finalizing the other components in your plan. This is where you will provide a high-level overview of the contents so that someone reading the summary will have a good idea of why the plan exists and what it will accomplish. For instance, you may have an executive team that has an interest in the marketing plan, but they lack the time to study the plan. It also provides a final review for the leadership team to summarize the vision. Since it is usually written last, it is one of the final chapters in this book.

Company positioning statement
This ties in tightly to your branding in the markets that you serve. Before you can position your brand, you need to take the time to be sure that you have these areas of your company defined. Do you have a mission

statement? If so, write it down at the beginning of your plan. All of your activities and experiences need to support your company's mission. What are the services that your company wants to provide? You may know how much revenue you want to achieve for the following year, but how are you going to achieve it? Keep it at a higher level. For instance, you may want to focus on roof replacement work with little focus on repairs and restoration. Or maybe your market has a growing demand for repair and maintenance and that is an area where your business will want to focus.

After understanding the services that you want to offer, what is your level of commitment to it? Will you need to invest in new or additional equipment? Will you need to hire more employees? Review the factors that will need to be addressed and spell it out at the beginning of the plan. This will guide you as you get into your strategic and yearly goals.

Lastly, as you understand the services and commitment level required think about what your unique value proposition is in those areas? This is simply defining what problem you can solve for your customer and how you can solve that problem differently or better than your competition.

Markets
What are the markets that you serve? Who is your ideal customer? Here is where you will identify the markets you want to be in and what products and services you want to offer to those markets. The things that define your market include geography, or where you want to do business; demographics, such as age, gender, income level, education level; and psychographics, including personality, attitudes, values and interests. The latter is sometimes referred to as a Buyer Persona. When you understand your target audience's needs and wants, your marketing messaging can be crafted to be especially powerful in that segment by hitting key points that are important to them.

Yearly goals and initiatives

Every business has goals and outlining them in your marketing plan will help you define the results that you need to achieve from your marketing efforts. There are two distinct kinds of goals to consider – strategic and tactical.

Strategic goals take the big picture into consideration. Here is where you will ask and answer the questions such as where you want your business to be in a year and if there are new services or products that you want to be able to offer. Looking at revenue targets is also a part of the strategic goals process. These considerations will be important factors in the development of your marketing plan and will be a key element in this section.

Tactical goals are how you plan to physically carry out the plan to achieve the strategic goals. The tactics are what you will use in your day-to-day operations to be successful. This could include advertising, public relations, digital campaigns, community service and many more activities. These tactics can be more clearly defined by breaking down your revenue goals and working backward to determine exactly how many leads need to be generated by your marketing activities. Tactical goals will be found in the meat of the plan under tools, tasks, timelines and budgets.

Every plan should also have special initiatives and messaging that are part of that year's campaigns. Each new year is a chance for fun new promotions, current and trendy messages and opportunities to support the community and employees. We will look at reviewing those opportunities during this section.

Branding
Branding is a critical part of your marketing plan. Your brand is your company's defining essence. It's what your company promises to deliver to its customers. So just what does your company deliver? You might say excellent service, quality roof installations and friendly staff. Those are all great things to deliver to your customer, but this is the time to dig a little

deeper and really come up with what your company can promise the customer that not every other roofing company offers.

In this piece of your marketing plan, you will define the brand experience you want your customers to have. This is the place where you will detail out how elements of your brand are incorporated throughout the customer journey from first contact with your business to finished project to your continued ongoing relationship.

Marketing tools
After setting goals, defining your market and developing your brand story, it's time to market your products and services. Here is where you will review all the avenues for reaching your identified market and decide what initiatives you will undertake to generate leads for your business. This will include reviewing items such as media outlets for print and digital opportunities, mailing campaigns, social media activities, local event participation, public relations opportunities, sponsorships and more.

Technology considerations
Anyone in business today should consider which technologies they need to have in place for success. Just as companies rely on software or cloud-based tools for invoicing and payroll, marketing and sales technologies exist to help with productivity and efficiency. This part of your plan will examine the technology tools, processes and operations related to sales and marketing that need to be added or upgraded for marketing success. As part of the evaluations you'll also determine what resources will be needed for successful implementation of the plan's activities.

Budget
After identifying the types of initiatives that you want to do, and the resources or tools needed to do it, the budget section is where you determine what everything will cost and set parameters for how much you want to spend on the marketing activities. Putting a detailed budget together will also be helpful in narrowing down which activities you will

implement. Budgets can be looked at as a percentage of revenue. They are also determined by the goals that you have set for the year. The budget should correlate to all goals and tools for the success of the business.

Tasks and timeline

A detailed task list and timeline should be developed for the marketing initiatives. This will keep you on track with the plan, but it also helps with the development of the budget and how expenses will come into play throughout the year.

Implementation and company communications

Now that your plan is put together, it's important to look at how it will be implemented. This will detail out who is going to take on what initiatives internally and identify external resources that will be needed for success. It will be very important to outline how you will communicate the plan to the rest of the employees in your company. Without the support and understanding of your employees, your plan will have less of a chance of success.

Your employees represent your brand out in the field, so it is critical that they understand the messaging that you will be putting into the marketplace. They also need to be aware of any ads, promotions, specials, etc. that will be marketed or advertised during the year so that if they are asked a question about something you are promoting, they won't be caught off guard.

Action items

1. Keep reading. The following chapters will provide action items or homework at the end of each chapter to develop your marketing plan.

Notes

CHAPTER 2

Company Positioning Statement

If you have a business plan, it is good to begin with what is in that document and incorporate it into the marketing plan. As discussed, marketing supports the company overall and all the departments within. Marketing can brand the company but putting together a company positioning statement needs to begin with the leadership team.

Incorporating what you already have in the business plan and then making sure it fits the current market environment is important. Reviewing your business plan with the leadership team is critical. Whether you already have a business plan or not, developing the company position statement is important to set the tone for overall marketing initiatives.

To develop a company positioning statement, it is good to take the leadership team through the following questions and discovery:

- What do we want to focus on next year?
- What did we do very well this year that we can continue and even improve for next year?
- What did we not do well? Should we discontinue or work at improving it?
- What markets are out there that we have not approached? Are we missing key business?
- Are we working in markets that are not profitable? Should we abandon them?

- What modern technologies are available that could change our market approach?

As the team works through the questions, be sure to record all of the thoughts. Large pieces of paper around the room that can be moved and consolidated is ideal. You will find that themes will emerge from the team that starts to create a direction for the new year.

From the discussion surrounding the above questions, the team will be able to pull out common themes and start to develop individual statements that may look like this:

- Commercial properties will be the target
- Energy saving roofing systems is a differentiator in the market and an excellent value proposition
- Service and maintenance with twice yearly on-roof inspections is the goal
- Customer service is a major selling point focused on strong communications, execution and responsiveness

From those statements, the team can start forming an overall statement that summarizes the direction. A company positioning statement can look something like this:

"ABC Roofing will focus on offering high-quality roofing systems that focus on energy savings for commercial properties. Our service teams will provide strong yearly service and maintenance options that not only service the roof but track energy savings through a partnership with local utilities. Through twice yearly service calls, we will deliver the best value and greatest security for our clients. We are focused on customer service that is well communicated, rapid in execution and responsive to the needs of our customers."

A company position statement is different than a mission statement. The idea of a yearly company positioning statement is what the company wants to do for that year. From a marketing position, the team will be able to start developing tactical goals.

In the upcoming chapters, we will dig deeper into customer evaluation, markets and setting goals. The team may find after working through the entire marketing plan that the company position statement may need to be changed or refined. Developing the statement at the beginning gives the leadership team a high-level look at the new year and is a great way to start the strategizing experience.

Action items

1. Work through the questions in this chapter with your leadership team, writing your answers below
    a. What do we want to focus on next year?

    b. What did we do very well this year that we can continue and even improve for next year?

    c. What did we not do well? Should we discontinue or work at improving it?

    d. What markets are out there that we have not approached? Are we missing key business?
    e. Are we working in markets that are not profitable? Should we abandon them?

    f. What new technologies are available that could change our market approach?

2. Write down everyone's views and begin consolidating with the common denominators

3. Make a list of the points for your company's position for the next year

4. Take the points and work them into a positioning statement, understanding that at the end of your plan you may need to come back and make changes due to items that are uncovered when building this marketing plan

Notes

Notes

CHAPTER 3

Understanding Your Markets

As you define your strengths and services, it is now time to overlap that with who needs those services. The formula for success is to tie your company's strengths to the right customers. For example, if low-slope installation is the sweet spot for your company, you are not going to want homeowner leads or projects.

When determining the best markets, you should consider locality, structure type, risk and materials needed. Looking at the review of the past year's jobs and creating a customer profile that fits your business will help to determine your target market for the upcoming year. For example, if retail work saw positive results, having the marketing efforts focus on shopping centers makes sense. Instead of spreading marketing dollars across many industries you can spend more in a smaller area and see targeted results.

A marketing plan is about understanding who your customers are and how to get in front of them; ultimately to sell your services. Understanding your market and customers takes time, research and a strong review of your company overall. It is really about understanding what your customers care about and matching your services to their needs or finding customers who need what you have to offer.

Here is where you might consider developing a buyer persona. Who is the person making the decision to purchase and what is important to them? If low-slope is the target for your business, and it is in retail, who makes the buying decision? Is it a facility manager or the shopping center leasing company? If it's the facility manager, they may want someone they know they can trust with after-hours headaches, so they don't miss their kids' sporting events. Or maybe they want someone who will make them look good in front of their boss. By understanding their pains, you can target your messaging to reinforce that you will be a great partner.

Who is your competition?
Most of you probably have a good idea of the kind of competition that you face in your area. While it's great that you have that information in your head, let's put it down on paper (or a spreadsheet) to create a quick reference guide. Create several columns that you can populate with information about your competition. Write down their name, the year they started, if they are licensed, what services they provide, list their web address and identify if they are actively marketing and where. Do you know their mission statement and their brand messaging? What are their strengths and their weaknesses?

Most of this information can be found through a visit to the company's website and through a Google search. This can also give you an idea of how well your company is ranking in online searches. Tuck that information away for later in the book.

Understanding the needs of the market
This is an essential element to identify. It might seem obvious but spell it out again in your plan. Different areas of the country prefer diverse types of roofs and you don't want to make the mistake of deciding to offer a product line or service that will have little to no traction.

You may be servicing a market that is located along major interstates where companies are increasingly building and positioning large product distribution centers. In that case, targeting the general contractors who are managing these projects would be a good fit.

If your focus is a residential market, keep in mind the ages of the neighborhoods, the average home price and the most popular roofing materials. You don't want to put a focus on specialty or higher end materials if the average price of the homes doesn't justify the high-end material.

Since every roofing business and every region of the country is different, with different niches and offerings, it's important to begin by identifying your markets and areas that you want to grow. Start by taking a piece of paper and making three columns on the sheet. Label the first one 'service to promote,' call the second one 'target markets' and the third column should be 'where do I reach them?' Your paper might end up looking like the graph in Appendix 2.

By taking the time to understand and write down information about your customers, competition and market, you are building the essential components of your marketing plan. This is a crucial step that needs to be done yearly. With technology and millennials changing how we do business, yearly review and strategy is essential.

Action items

1. Identify your strengths and the services you want to offer to which markets

2. Define your buyer – residential and/or commercial

3. Who are your competitors and what services do they offer?

4. Outline the needs of your markets

5. Identify where the best place is to reach your market

Notes

Notes

CHAPTER 4

Yearly Goals and Initiatives

Setting goals for your organization and employees is critical to the success of any business or marketing plan. Without goals and expected results, plans may just gather dust, never really making an impact or difference in the organization. According to studies, 76% of organizations who successfully monitor and meet original goals and business intent see overall business success compared to only 38% of companies succeeding without strong goals and expectations.

As part of reviewing goals, marketing requirements need to include many different areas of goal setting which include markets, sales objectives, divisional/department priorities and overall company initiatives. Marketing plans should support all functions of a company no matter the size. Often marketing is thought of as only supporting sales, but, it should play an integral role in building the overall brand for the company and every department or division within the company.

To set and then execute company goals, a review is critical. Following are questions that should be addressed by the leadership team and potentially the company as a whole. By including employees, you may learn valuable information from various parts of the company that will not only help with planning and goal setting but also provide an opportunity to make necessary changes now.

What does your company do well?

This may seem obvious to some, but many contractors look at their market with the goal of just getting any roofing job possible. Most companies have specialties which can include low-slope or steep-slope roofing, insurance work, commercial or residential roofing. Few companies can do all types of roofing well. Successful companies continue to focus their operations and crews on projects that deliver high quality installations with good margins.

With your leadership team evaluate the work accomplished over the last year. During the evaluation look at profitability per job, customer reviews, crew satisfaction and overall success. You may see that certain jobs were good for crews but were not profitable or maybe they were profitable but did not receive good customer reviews. Ideally, they should receive positive installation results, customer satisfaction and profitability that helps to grow the company.

If the results are not positive, this is the time to evaluate services, sales, crews and products. What caused poor profitability, reviews or company culture? Is it the type of work, the type of customers or how the crews interface with the products? If operations have been focused on low-slope work and then are required to begin working steep-slope, it may cause employee disgruntlement along with loss of profitability. You need to figure out what is happening in the field or sales office that is losing the company money.

Through the review you may also find mediocre results; not bad but not great. This is an opportunity to tweak operations and to move installations and customer satisfaction towards great results. And if the results are already great, it makes it even easier to set realistic goals for the upcoming year.

Setting Goals

Once the review has been completed and addressed it is time to set goals for the upcoming year. It is recommended to look at goals overall from a high-level company perspective and then push down more tactical goals to each department. Sales will be all about revenue, but what are the goals of the marketing team? Ideally, they will help support the goals of each department. Operations may focus on safety. Keeping employees safe and safety fines at a minimum is an important goal financially and culturally. It will be important to budget time and money from marketing to help with promoting internal programs.

But the company goals are the place to start. For example, the goals may look like the following:

- Increase profitability by _____% overall.
- Enter retail market with a focus on low-slope work
- Add energy roofing solutions for building owners
- Increase closing rates by _____%
- Grow company revenue overall by _____%

With those company goals in mind, determine what every department needs to do to contribute to those goals. It may look like this for the profitability goal:

- Financial – Work with suppliers and distributors for best material buying options
- Operations – Focus on safety that enhances productivity while understanding new energy technology
- Marketing – Target high-end homeowners that focus on quality products and installation and building owners focused on energy savings through new systems, service and maintenance

- Sales – Focus on the right estimates to the right customers to deliver profitable jobs while delivering new information for energy saving options

For every company goal, there should be matching departmental goals. This allows employees to be a part of the process. Monthly check point meetings should review how the goals are being met and what may need to be tweaked. In the end, marketing should be able to support each department by not only helping with internal programs but creating campaigns that generate leads that fit the goals of the company.

The goals that are set will then be reflected in the marketing plan showing how marketing will support each department and overall company goals. Tactical plans can be linked to the goals with budget, task and timeline to allow everyone in the company to succeed.

Action items

1. List what you do well then dive in for a deep understanding of your company numbers and profitability.

2. What are your company goals for the upcoming year?

3. List what each department needs to do in order to meet the overall company goals. Remember it isn't just additional sales that contribute to profitability.

Notes

CHAPTER 5

Branding

Your brand is much more than just a name and a logo. Your brand defines who you are and what kind of experience you want to deliver to your clients. It's your company's personality and voice. It can also be what sets you apart from your competition. It is a critical part of your marketing plan. For some it may be brand new while for others may involve rebranding. Branding should be evaluated every year. It is an integral part of any marketing plan.

If you've been in business for a few years, you might want to start with a simple brand audit. Find out what people think of your brand and what is important to your customers. Your sales team interacts with those customers every day. Have them ask what's important to the customer when working with a roofing company in addition to identifying their concerns and expectations.

Next, look at your logo. How does it make you feel? What do you think of first when you see it? Is it fresh and appealing or is it dated and in need of an update? Most companies freshen up their logo after so many years. If you search online for 'company logo evolution' you will see examples of famous companies and how they have updated their logos throughout the years.

After getting feedback about how your brand is perceived by customers, you can decide or re-evaluate what your brand promise is or is going to be. Your brand promise is simply what your company promises to deliver to its customers. You might decide that your brand delivers quality roof installations, excellent customer service and friendly staff. Those are all important things to deliver to your customers but it's important to define exactly what those things mean. This is how you differentiate your brand and company from your competitors.

To help you understand a brand promise and what it means for your business, we'll look throughout this chapter at the fictitious company ABC Roofing. ABC Roofing's brand promise is: "ABC Roofing promises to provide a professional, quality installation safely, on time, with as little disruption as possible and stand behind the installation."

Remember that a brand promise is serious. When you make a promise to your customer they develop certain expectations surrounding that promise. If you fail to deliver, customers will be let down, become confused and will begin to seek satisfaction elsewhere, from another brand. By documenting the progression of your logo and brand promise in the marketing plan, the leadership team can track how it is working. Whenever there are large changes, those updates need to be key in the new year marketing initiatives.

Integrate and differentiate
We wrote about this next section in our last book, *Sales and Marketing for Roofing Contractors*, but it's so important that it bears repeating. Your brand should be evident in everything you do, right down to how your staff answers the phone. Employees are your brand ambassadors and it's important for them to understand and agree with the brand promise.

There are plenty of contractors who can install and service a roof, but you differentiate your business through the integration of your brand promise throughout your customer's experience. Let's examine how to integrate a brand promise into a business. If you recall, our fictitious company, ABC Roofing, developed a brand promise of:

"ABC Roofing promises to provide a professional, quality installation safely, on time, with as little disruption as possible and stand behind the installation."

The first promise is to be professional. ABC Roofing has defined professional to mean:
- employees wear apparel with company logos and have ID badges
- trucks and vehicles are clean inside and out and bear the company logo
- no smoking on the jobsite
- booties are placed over shoes before entering customers' homes

The second part of the promise is to deliver a "quality installation, safely and on time." This is defined as:
- Being certified to install various manufacturers' products and system
- Taking advantage of ongoing training and learning opportunities
- Always adhering to OSHA rules and standards without cutting corners
- Showing up to start the job when promised

"With as little disruption as possible" is the next promise. ABC Roofing delivers on this by reviewing aerial photos of the home with the homeowner to determine the best areas for material delivery, dumpster positioning, access points and delicate landscaping to avoid. The company also asks questions about what to be aware of, such as if there are children that will be arriving home from school in the middle of the day.

Lastly, ABC Roofing has promised to "stand behind the installation." Most contractors will say they stand behind their installation, but ABC Roofing goes a step further and provides a six month and one-year inspection at no cost to the customer. Not only does this send a strong message to the homeowner, it allows the company to have continued contact with them and provides an opportunity to sell an ongoing inspection and maintenance program at the end of the first year.

Consistency
Now that you have defined your brand promise and decided how it will be integrated throughout your business and marketing plans, you need to make sure that your team is consistent in its use. Developing a brand guideline manual will ensure that no one jeopardizes the integrity of your brand. A brand guideline manual can be as short as a one-page document or can consist of several pages.

The brand guideline should contain the company official name and how it should be used in various situations such as formal communications, advertising, sales presentations, social media, and in speaking. The guideline will also demonstrate proper use of the company logo and should designate the company's brand (or PMS) colors for use by printers and other vendors. This will ensure that the colors are always correct and there is no risk of distortion or misrepresentation to your logo.

You might want to consider spelling out the acceptable colors for your logo when it is being used on promotional giveaway items or being embroidered onto clothing. There are cases where if the specified logo colors are used, it won't be as visible, depending on the color of the item.

For instance, if your main logo color is a dark, navy blue and you want to order black polo shirts, the logo will be very hard to see. In this case, a contrasting color such as grey or silver would be appropriate to use. By designating that ahead of time in the brand guideline, you will be certain that there will be no surprises when ordering clothing.

The brand guide is a separate document from your marketing plan but should be included in overall marketing documentation for your company.

Employees as Brand Ambassadors

It is important to engage your employees as your brand ambassadors. They represent your brand every day in their interactions out in the community and with customers. Employees are one of your best marketing tools but only if they are engaged and believe in the work they are doing. Include how you will incorporate employees in the marketing plan and then share it with the entire team.

Here is how you and your management team can encourage your employees to become brand ambassadors:

- **It starts with asking for their opinion.** Don't just ask them to promote the business but ask for their feedback on what they believe are the company's strongest assets and where there may be room for improvement. By including them in the process of improving the company they gain ownership for the overall enterprise, gaining pride and confidence.

- **Create channels of communication.** Be sure your employees know what is going on within the company. Take the time to educate and get them excited about new products, projects or services that make your company distinctive. Include them on company newsletter mailings or emails. Make it easy for them to share the excitement.

- **Encourage social media interaction and advocacy.** This is an area that is still hard for many companies. Is the employee engaged or just scrolling through Facebook? In this day and age, it is both. Employees live their lives at work and at home. They are liking posts, commenting on new information and making referrals. How powerful is it when they do it for their own place of work?

- **Allow employees to help strengthen customer relationships.** Every positive meeting is a great sales and marketing opportunity for the company. Whether it is accounting, jobsite production, sales or the front desk, employees should leave the customer smiling and happy. Employees need the time to introduce themselves and be a part of fixing or improving the process. It is ok to ask for referrals after a good experience, but it takes every employee being an amazing brand ambassador to create that perfect referral and sustainable business model.

- **Financially and emotionally encourage involvement.** Help employees be involved in professional and community associations. Having employees attend Chamber of Commerce events, sponsoring school sports or helping with community service projects gives them the time to advocate for their place of work while being involved. It shows that the company is committed to the community it works in and is willing to support their employees' involvement.

- **Make sharing easy.** Help employees share this information with each other and your customers. Monthly lunch and learns that share how to be a brand ambassador, social media discussion groups and company newsletters are all ways to engage and educate employees. Encourage employees to follow the company on all social media. These exercises can make a huge difference in building morale, commitment and helping employees message the uniqueness of the company!

- **Make sure every employee is enabled to be a brand ambassador.** From the rooftop to the front desk, every employee should be able to talk about the mission and differentiating qualities of the company. Why is this the best roofing and exterior contracting company? What do we offer that is different? How can our employees help create raving fans or amazing customer brand ambassadors?

By taking these steps, asking questions and taking the time to train employees on the company's brand, marketing materials and messaging it will reap great rewards including a commitment to make the most of every minute. Make your employees a part of the mission and brand of your company. Share how important employee engagement is and it will not only help the company but will help your employees own personal performance and future financial success.

This is all part of a marketing plan. You may think it is just advertising campaigns, but it is everything including your logo, messaging and employee engagement. By bringing all of this into your marketing plan you can stay on task of creating the company that you desire with marketing materials, initiatives and planning that will make it happen.

Action items

1. Ask employees who interact with customers what they think customers think of your brand. What do you think is being said in the field?

2. Define your brand promise and experience and spell out exactly what that means.

3. List the steps that are necessary to turn your employees into brand ambassadors (include the topic as a standing agenda item in your weekly team meetings).

Notes

Notes

CHAPTER 6

Marketing Tools and Initiatives

Depending on your business model you may need to develop several different marketing programs. Take a look at the divisions within your company. You might offer commercial roofing, residential roofing and offer maintenance and repair programs. In that case the messaging to each of your target markets that you identified earlier will be marketed to differently.

Programs by Division
A commercial roofing and maintenance division will want to market to building owners, facility managers and even build relationships with consultants, architects and engineers. The messaging to these audiences is very different than it will be to a residential market where your focus is homeowners.

You might also want to target specific segments within a market. For instance, you may install a high-end residential product where you only want to target homeowners with properties valued at more $300,000. Or you may have discovered that on the commercial side of your business you've excelled at repair, maintenance and roof replacements on shopping centers and want to focus efforts on commercial real estate firms. As discussed earlier, determining your focus areas and who you want to reach is critical before deciding the tactical goals of your marketing efforts.

Now that you have identified what services you want to promote and grow, who you will promote them to and where to find your target markets, we can look at some of the tools you will need to implement your marketing plans.

Logos

With the evolution of technology and the internet, it's easier than ever to find a designer to help with your brand and any updates that you might need. There are sites online, such as DesignCrowd and 99Designs where you can provide information about your needs, set a budget for what you are willing to pay, and designers will compete by submitting their design ideas. In some cases, you'll end up with 20 or 30 ideas for just a few hundred dollars.

Digital Marketing

One of the things that all your target markets have in common is that they all can be reached online, so it's important to have some digital marketing plans in place. While digital marketing may sound intimidating, there are tools available that make it very easy for you to implement some basic plans such as email marketing and online advertising.

Start with an email marketing program. There are many online email marketing services available including Constant Contact, MailChimp and even GoDaddy offers that service now. Some are free to get started (as of this writing, MailChimp was free if you have fewer than 2,000 email addresses). Many offer features such as marketing automation which allows you to automatically send emails in specific situations.

For instance, if someone completes a form on your website to request service, your email program can send them an automatic thank you email. Be sure to consider if the email program that you choose will integrate into any existing software you are using to operate your business, such as a customer relationship management program.

Next, decide what kind of emails you will send. A good mix includes thank you emails, appointment confirmation emails, inquiry acknowledgement emails and you might want to consider developing a quarterly email newsletter that offers tips, reminders and a promotional offer such as a discounted service.

Your business probably already has a lot of email addresses collected from working with customers over the last few years and attending home shows or other industry events. Consider hiring an intern to help with data entry by reviewing files and gathering email addresses to be entered into your email database.

We can't stress enough the importance of working with a reputable email service such as one of the ones mentioned previously. They will ensure that your business is in compliance with the anti-spam laws (CAN-SPAM Act) that was enacted in 2003. Violators (or spammers) can be fined tens of thousands of dollars in fines for each email recipient that received an email. Don't put your business at risk by trying to do it yourself.

Another key component to a good digital marketing program is to be sure your website is up-to-date, optimized to be found in search engines and that you are pushing fresh content on a regular basis. You also want to have a social media presence as part of the strategy. For customers to find you, you need to be where they are.

The following questions should help you answer whether your website needs attention:

- **Do I have a website?** If not, put this book down right now and don't come back until you have one.
- **When was my website created?** Has it been updated since then? If your site hasn't been reviewed in more than two years, it's time to have a professional look at it. Google updates search

algorithms every few months and this is where a professional is necessary to ensure your site will be found favorably in searches.
- **Do I have a clear, effortless way for customers to contact me on my website?** There should be an easy contact form and a link to it from every page that allows people needing your services to get in touch with you. Also, be sure that you have a policy in place for prompt follow up to every inquiry.
- **Do I have an e-newsletter sign up option on my site?** Whether you have developed one yet or not, start capturing email addresses at every opportunity.
- **Is my website mobile optimized?** With 50 percent or more of people using smartphones and tablets to search for information, a mobile-optimized site is a must – not only in the eyes of Google, which ranks mobile-friendly sites higher, but also for your customers to have a valuable experience.
- **Is the content on my site relevant, fresh and informative?** Having the right content and keywords in the copy on your website certainly helps you rank higher in search results, but search engines have gotten smarter over the years. They can tell when someone is just dumping a bunch of keywords onto a page to try to fool the system. It won't work and may, in fact, hurt you. This is an area where it can be important to engage an expert.

Now that you have asked yourself these questions about your website, you should know if you need to do some work on it before you begin driving leads to your site.

Social Media

If your business is not on social media, set up accounts as soon as possible. A recent Pew Research Study showed that up to 68 percent of U.S. adults are on Facebook alone (http://www.pewinternet.org/fact-sheet/social-media/) with 76 percent of those users using it daily. This is great news if your target market is homeowners. Commercial contractors shouldn't be discouraged though. Their audience can typically be found on Twitter and LinkedIn. Those two platforms combined have a nearly 50 percent reach into the U.S. adult market.

Don't be intimidated by establishing an online presence through these channels. If you aren't out there now, you better believe your competitors are and they will likely beat you to the customer. So many companies are hiring millennials to be a part of their teams and this generation grew up with social media. They know it well, inside and out. Ask a millennial on your team to help you.

Another great thing about social media is that it's free for anyone to create an account. The reason that it remains free is because they make their money from advertisers. And you should consider becoming an advertiser on a social media platform. What's great about it is that people are telling you their age, their likes, where they live, where they work, what their interests are and more. This makes targeting the right demographic easier than it's ever been in the history of marketing and advertising!

Most social media users don't mind seeing ads for services and/or products that they deem relevant to their current situation. If you are targeting facility managers on LinkedIn after a particularly severe weather event or more-than-average rainy season with maintenance and restoration services, that could be very relevant to their situation with the buildings they are managing.

Targeting ads by online behaviors
Anytime you are online researching products or solutions, checking your social media accounts or looking for information on that industry conference you are thinking about attending, you are leaving a digital footprint. It's like a trail of breadcrumbs about where you have been, but in the case of the internet they are called cookies. By using a website, you are agreeing to their use of cookies. A cookie is a unique identifier or bit

of data that is placed within your web browser, so a website remembers you when you come back and can see your interests and interactions.

Have you ever looked at a product on Amazon and then the next day, you see an ad for that very product while you are checking the day's weather? Cookies are wonderful treats for advertisers. You can take advantage of them too and target people with ads based on sites they visit, words they search for and products they view.

This differs from Google AdWords. With Google AdWords, you bid on certain search terms in specific geographic areas (such as your service area) and pay a dollar amount based on each click that you receive. We rank AdWords as a very important digital marketing tool – especially for home improvement contractors – but recommend engaging an expert to manage this who is familiar with the industry.

That is worth repeating – an expert who is familiar with the industry. There are many AdWords management services that will gladly take your money each month but don't have the experience and understanding of what it takes to convert a home improvement click into a lead. Do your due diligence and ask for referrals. Investigate the company as well. Many will throw up a website claiming to specialize in Roofing AdWords but upon further investigation you find they are targeting every industry out there.

Community Relations
While digital marketing initiatives are pretty exciting, there are some things that never go out of style. Let's take a look at good old community relations. This is, simply put, your and your employees' involvement in the local community. Go through these simple activities to see how engaged your business is in the community:

- List out which employees are members of a civic or community organization like Jaycees, Kiwanis or Rotary.

- Which of your employees is a youth sports coach?
- Which of your employees is a boy or girl scout leader?
- Who at your company volunteers for a non-profit organization?
- Who attends your local AIA or ABC chapter meetings?

As we've said in earlier articles and books, people do business with people they like and trust. Consider this: Joe is one of your better salespeople and has developed great working relationships with general contractors and facility managers over the years. They know Joe and trust him and your company's work. How did Joe establish those relationships? He did it by being involved in industry and community associations. He went to meetings, he volunteered his time, he was in situations where he was able to share his expertise. Over the years, he built trust and camaraderie. It's a win-win situation to support your team's involvement in these associations and organizations.

Lead generation
These activities that you've read about from having a website, to sending emails to targeted ads online to participating in the local community all share a common goal: to generate leads for your business. Each needs to be evaluated to determine if it will work in your market. Marketing plans are about pairing the right tactics with the overall goals and it may not work the first time. Documentation along with trial and error will determine what is best for your business and your marketing plan.

Special initiatives and messaging
Every year should also have special initiatives and messaging that are part of that year's campaigns. It is a chance for fun new promotions, current and trendy messages and opportunities to support the community and employees. The leadership team should look to the culture of the company to find initiatives that fit.

There are several areas that can be highlighted through non-traditional marketing. Take time as a team to discuss and review the following questions:

- Does ownership or employees have a special community service program?
- What are the current needs of the community and how can the company help?
- What is important to your customers? Can you partner with them on special projects?
- What is trending on social media or in the community? How can the company be a part of that?
- Culturally, what do employees get involved in and how can you support their interests?
- Can you include customers, vendors and employees in chosen initiatives?

Once you have discussed these questions, think about pushing the questions out past the leadership team to your employees overall. Get their feedback and understand how combining marketing initiatives, community service and your employees' interests together can be a win-win-win.

Once the initiatives are chosen, it is time to put the concepts and ideas down on paper. Be sure to plan them out so they are organized and promoted. This offers you an opportunity to publicize the programs and get community support along with customer attention. It is something your sales team can talk about with clients. It is ok to share your community involvement, also known as cause marketing. It creates a win for everyone.

Finally, be sure to allocate funds for new or unexpected initiatives or promotions. It should be part of the marketing budget and reflect the commitment to the program. By investing in the community and your employees, you will see a good return on investment from new customers and revenue growth of current customers. They like to do business with good people who care.

Action items

1. What marketing tools do you currently have in place?

2. What tools will your business need to succeed?

3. List out your social media accounts and identify opportunity for improvement

4. List out employees who are involved in the community

5. Write down special initiative opportunities in your community that you can support and involve employees as well

6. Develop a communications plan and allocate budget dollars for special initiatives

Notes

CHAPTER 7

Technology Considerations

In today's world, where efficiency and precision take precedence, technology is a key component when it comes to doing business within the contracting community. Technology comes in many shapes and sizes, but leading contractors are realizing that if they are not progressive in their use of technology they are going to be left behind. It must become part of your business and marketing planning.

Technology is not just software, it is using services and cloud-based solutions to help increase productivity for the company and employees. Exploring multiple types of technology and evaluating their effectiveness for a roofing company, no matter the size or type, can play an important part in the growth of a business.

Innovative technologies and applications are introduced literally every day. Understanding what is beneficial for a roofing business and, more importantly, the best technology for the size of the business is critical for success. Here are a few important sales and marketing technologies that should be evaluated and potentially incorporated into your marketing plans.

Smart Devices
It does not seem possible to survive in today's world without a smart device and that is especially true when it comes to business. Smart phones allow contractors to be in touch immediately with their

customers, giving them the edge when it comes to customer service. The agility of utilizing smart phones makes sense for communication with other employees while providing the overall benefit of informed customers.

As you review tools for your business and marketing planning, it is important to use phones in a way that works with customers, so knowing their preferences concerning email, text or phone usage is beneficial for creating enhanced communications. As part of the sales process, ask how the customer would prefer to receive their project communications. A critical part of utilizing technology is understanding how customers want to interact with that technology.

In deciding which smart device to use, take the time to coordinate the company's phones, tablets and computer system with cloud-based software in a way that all devices can speak to each other. This creates an easy, efficient means of transferring data and documents while also documenting customer discussions.

Customer Relationship Management
There are several Customer Relationship Management (CRM) systems designed for roofing professionals that can help you accomplish improved customer communications and work with other systems to ensure that your company's smart devices and computers are in sync. CRM systems have evolved significantly over the years from server-based systems such as ACT to simple contact management solutions such as Microsoft Outlook or Excel to cloud-based, enterprise-level software like Salesforce. In the roofing world, there are many contractor CRM software systems that help manage customers. They are often also connected to project management and/or accounting software.

A strong CRM is essential for your marketing program. Digital marketing is how we will be marketing in the future and maintaining and understanding the data that is generated online is key to strong customer relations, prospecting and ongoing referrals.

Questions to ask when looking for a CRM system include how the program works for residential vs. commercial business. Ideally it will handle both. There are companies that are very focused on residential projects with functionalities that track canvassing, sales and overall leads. Commercial roofing software may focus more on inspections, service and maintenance and may feature a customer portal that allows property owners to access service records and to request maintenance online.

Depending on the business model of the roofing company, residential, commercial or both, the CRM needs to fit the business. As roofing companies continue to grow and gain sophistication, an essential element for any CRM systems is the ability to track customer's overall data and retain that data for long-term use.

No matter the CRM chosen, the key is to maintain a strong, up-to-date customer database that becomes not only a historical view of customers and projects but also a strong database for future sales and marketing. This will require funding for either an employee or outsourced group to maintain the database and eventually implement marketing automation. Be sure to create a section within the marketing plan and budget that addresses digital marketing and customer data.

Marketing Automation
There are multiple buzzwords in the marketing world and currently one of the biggest is *Marketing Automation*. The question many are asking is "What is it?" According to Marketing Automation Times, an online publication, marketing automation is a subset of customer relationship management (CRM) that focuses on the definition, scheduling, segmentation and tracking of marketing campaigns. The use of marketing automation makes processes that would otherwise have been performed manually much more efficient and makes new processes possible.

That defin tion is just the tip of the iceberg. Yes, it is about automating processes such as email, blogs and web tracking but it is also about building relationships with customers and potential customers that change the dynamic from chasing leads to attracting leads.

For residential and commercial roofing contractors, there is an ongoing need to not only attract customers but to sustain them over long periods of time. Whether it is homeowners or building owners, they need to be nurtured so that your company stays top of mind for when they have roofing needs or for when they are giving a referral.

There are many companies that will provide marketing automation services. They usually combine it with other services such as email marketing, downloadable content and search engine optimization (SEO). SEO involves a thorough review of the content on your website, which is how Google or other search engines determine where you show up in search results. The better optimized your site is with relevant information, the higher you will appear in the results; with the goal being to show up on the first page.

While evaluating services, be sure to interview several companies. Reach out to associations to see what types of discounted programs they may offer or recommend. Often marketing organizations outside of the construction industry do not understand the difference in marketing between homeowners and building owners, residential or commercial. In talking to other contractors, associations or vendors, contractors can get recommendations for good service providers that have delivered results for other companies.

Implementing Automation
There are many online companies that offer a full software solution for tracking activity on websites, sending emails and linking it all with social media. In locking at this type of technology, be sure your company is

ready for new processes and increased lead generation. It's important to connect your CRM to the marketing automation system so you can understand how the content that is being sent out through email, social media or online correlates to your sales efforts. Leads will increase with this type of marketing, so it is important to put time and resources in place to handle the return.

There are agencies who offer marketing automation services. Again, make time to vet their services and ensure they understand the roofing business. To implement this type of software, finding good agencies, consultants or freelancers can help with the learning curve. Just as your customers call you as the roofing expert, it's equally important that you consult with experts in marketing who understand your industry.

Marketing automation is a strong software tool to communicate with customers electronically. But, it is just one part of building good relationships through sales and marketing. Some companies have allowed technology to swing the pendulum too far away from personal relationships. Marketing electronically is about staying top of mind, but it is only a small part of building strong relationships of trust with customers.

Combining electronic communication with person-to-person communications can create exceptional customer satisfaction, referrals and highly sustainable business for roofing companies. Using marketing automation as one of the tools in a marketing program and linking it to the overall goals and strategies is the winning combination. Addressing the balance of technology and relationship selling is important in the marketing plan so that you keep a balance when communicating with customers and prospects.

Customer Portals
For current customers, it is important to continually delight them by creating exceptional customer experiences. Leading contractors are using

CRM programs that offer customer portals where they share data, photos, job progress, inspections and invoices with customers at their convenience. This type of CRM can be used for initial customer contact and sales along with the ability to track customers over time while storing all projects and related data.

Customer portals create an excellent user experience for customers. Innovative, web-based software systems are utilizing relational database programs to efficiently help contractors manage everything from project data, work order/invoicing processes and most importantly customer communication and document storage.

Many facility managers are asking for this type of communication. It offers a 24/7 ability to see what is happening with service, maintenance and re-roofing projects. Maintenance portals play a significant role for facility managers, allowing them to see exactly what is happening on their roofs. Understanding that very few managers will have the opportunity to walk all their roofs, portals provide a view of the roof that inspires confidence through ongoing communications, documentation and visual review. Data storage and the ability to upload unlimited photos or video to the portal is essential in providing real-time documentation for customers.

There is a strong opportunity for residential contractors to offer the same portals to homeowners. By making home repair information available 24/7 to homeowners they can be active with the contractor and their home improvements. Implementing technology that retains all data on a property over time provides an excellent means of retaining homeowner business with ongoing repairs, yearly inspections and potential upgrades.

By working outside of the norm, it also helps to differentiate your company. Note that today, there are many portals out there from medical to financial. Consumers are getting used to them. A marketing plan that includes a portal view for customers can be unique, creating opportunities for new business and a reason to make current customers stickier.

Evaluation of Technology
The most important part of incorporating any technology is to take the time to evaluate. Talk to other contractors through roofing associations or networks and see what has worked for them. Look at online reviews and utilize free trials to try out and understand the technology. There is a large commitment in time whenever there is a change or adoption of modern technology, so be sure it is matches the goals of the company.

Also, be aware that many types of software adoption will have a cultural effect on the company. Processes will need to be updated, personnel trained, and data uploaded. It is not easy to change software so create a relationship with the software provider upfront and develop a high degree of comfort and confidence when initiating the new technology and processes with employees.

It is worth the time to find the right systems to not only grow your company but improve productivity and profitability.

Action items

1. Write down all current hardware and software that your company is using and evaluate its success. Is it doing the job? Does it fit the company culture, processes and operations? Do you need to make a change or just tweak it?

2. What are you missing? Do you need more mobile devices in the field or better marketing software or equipment?

3. Is the technology you are currently utilizing keeping up with the competition?

4. How is the overall customer experience when it comes to utilizing technology? Do you need to incorporate more progressive technology or work on internal processes?

5. Document any software or equipment that will help sales and marketing with their marketing plan and budget. Determine how technology will play a part in the marketing program's initiatives.

Notes

Notes

CHAPTER 8

Budgeting

As we have discussed before, when it comes to budgeting you need to review your current year-to-date financials. How have you done with marketing this year? Are you over or under budget? Do you have a budget? Tracking dollars that are spent on marketing is very important. Having a budget makes that tracking process much easier.

Let's start with those who may not have a marketing budget. It is important to identify what has been spent on marketing to help build a budget for the next year. This is going to include everything you do to brand and market your company to the public.

Categories may include:
- Printing and collateral production (for truck magnets, door hangers, etc.)
- Memberships (associations and civic groups)
- Home shows (exhibit space and graphics production)
- Subscriptions (email software, services)
- Freelancers (website creation/maintenance, graphic design, writing)
- Technology costs (website, social media, CRM)
- Digital and traditional advertising (AdWords, TV, radio)

There may be additional categories that fit your business so take the time to pull together everything you have spent that helps you communicate with your customers. Once you have looked at the past, take the time to look at the future. Gather your leadership team and talk about the new year and what you hope to accomplish; are you adding new services, does your brand need a facelift with new graphics or website, will you need to hire a marketing coordinator. By reviewing future goals, you can start creating an overall budget to support those plans.

In our many years of marketing, we have often been asked the question of 'what percentage of gross revenue should be allocated to marketing expenses?' There are averages out there, but the answer is that it depends. It depends on the offering and the market. We've seen plans that are doing the bare minimum at three percent of gross revenue to companies releasing new products or services that are allocating eight or 10 percent of revenue toward marketing. There is no set answer because there are so many variables.

A residential roofing lead might have a higher cost per acquisition than a commercial roofing lead because home improvement services are abundant in your market. Or the opposite could be possible. Your past spending can serve as a guideline. If your marketing hasn't produced the results you want, it might be time to not only evaluate the messaging and outlets but the budget as well.

As the marketing budget comes together, there may be an overall concern on how you are going to make this work. There are many ways to creatively fund your marketing budget for overall success. Right now, as you are working on your marketing budget, so are your manufacturers and distributors. They are looking at certified contractor programs, reward programs and business building opportunities.

If you are already signed up, do not forget to take advantage of your year-end rewards. As we have worked with contractors and manufacturers in the past, we have seen where thousands of dollars have been left on the table by roofing contractors. Every major manufacturer has programs for business building support, but many contractors simply do not ask for it, nor do they follow-up with the paperwork. It is worth the time to look at what type of marketing tools and services are provided. In fact, it is not just at the end of the year when these are available. Your marketing budget can be supplemented all year long by using manufacturer services, discounts and opportunities.

Talk to your suppliers about cooperative advertising (co-op) programs that will contribute dollars toward marketing initiatives that include their logo. There are different guidelines for what is covered and there might be reporting required but this is free marketing money. In many co-op programs, contractors earn dollars based on material purchases or warranties sold. These same programs will often see those dollars expire at the end of the year. Don't be one of the contractors that leaves dollars sitting on the table.

There are also manufacturers that will design and provide co-branded materials for you to use in presentations and marketing efforts. They may offer technology to support your needs including SEO services, website support, sales apps and much more. All you need to do is ask your sales representative and they can give you details of their program.

Finally, be sure to look to all your local vendors for the best value. Notice I did not say best price. Marketing and advertising can be expensive but there are many ways to supplement what you are doing with "value ads." Value ads include free extras that can help promote your message and brand further than traditional advertising. An example would be if you advertise with TV or radio, what else can they do besides the ads? Ask about video production, events and sponsorships. They should also have an active web and social media presence where they can highlight your company. Look at what other advertisers are doing and ask for the same.

Budgeting is critical for marketing success. Through the budgeting process, you can really take the time to think about what you want and how you are going to accomplish it. Including an opportunity fund is a good idea for additional marketing needs that may arise after your budget is complete. This provides the needed flexibility for a strong marketing program.

Action items

1. Gather all marketing expenses from the past year.

2. List out new programs or additional needs and determine costs

3. Create an excel document for the budget that can be updated as you go through the year

4. Work closely with accounting department in order to deliver a strong, functional budget

Notes

Notes

CHAPTER 9

Tasks and Timeline

A detailed task list and timeline should be developed for the marketing initiatives. This will keep you on track with the plan, but it also helps with the development of the budget and how expenses will come into play throughout the year.

Tasks and timelines are critical for success. Start on a high level by listing all of your marketing initiatives. The following table shows the simplicity of listing your projects. The dates are meant to be an indicator of the time of year to start the initiative.

Dates can move but it is important to understand the relevance of when you need to launch the new website for instance. The beginning of the year is a perfect time to share a new look and information with your customers. It is best not to launch initiatives and marketing around holidays or when you know your customers may be distracted with local activities.

Also review how the different marketing functions work with each other. If you are launching a new website, then you will also need to have blog content and an editorial calendar for that blog ready. Having articles prepared for a couple of months is a good idea. Understanding how the initiatives work together and affect each other will help you implement successful marketing programs.

We recommend developing an excel document or use online project management program like Basecamp to track your projects and stay on task. It is easy to create the marketing plan, budget, tasks and timelines and let them sit in a filing cabinet. The plan and especially the tasks need to be reviewed monthly if not weekly to make sure that all the initiatives are taking shape and being executed successfully.

The successful execution of the tasks on timeline needs to be shared monthly with the leadership team and reviewed regularly with the sales team. The sales team will be able to use current marketing initiatives as talking points with customers and share the programs with prospects. By working together, it will create leads and opportunities on a regular basis that can be closed.

Finally, be sure to share sales and marketing success with the company overall. Quarterly updates are great. They can be shared at company meetings, on bulletin boards or online. Be sure to share the campaigns as they are happening. As discussed, this creates excellent consistency in messaging from all employees to customers. Then sharing the success of each campaign validates the time, budget and importance of organized and effective marketing.

See Appendix 3 for a first quarter sample task and timeline that you can use for your marketing initiatives.

Action items

1. Create an excel document listing all campaigns, tasks involved and projected completion date

2. Look at potential online project management tools for enhanced team communications

3. Create reporting for leadership team as initiatives are completed and the results

4. Review and understand how initiatives will work together and time needed to successfully implement

Notes

CHAPTER 10

Executive Summary

Don't be intimidated by the Executive Summary. Sometimes when you put the word executive in front of something it makes you feel like it's going to be something fancy - take executive suite for instance, or the executive level of an office building.

In the case of a marketing plan, the executive summary is just a summary or a quick read for your leadership team. The purpose it serves is to provide an understanding of the marketing activities that will be taking place throughout the coming year, without getting into the technical aspects of how the activities will be carried out or who will be managing the day-to-day activities related to the marketing plan.

You may already have a head start on developing your executive summary if you have begun thinking about an internal launch event for your employees (covered in the next chapter). It will be very similar to that high-level presentation of activities but will likely have some more figures and goal-oriented details.

Start with a review of your company positioning statement that you developed in chapter two of this book. For ABC Roofing, we determined that our positioning statement was:

"ABC Roofing will focus on offering high quality roofing systems that focus on energy savings for commercial properties. Our service teams will provide strong yearly service and maintenance options that not only service the roof but track energy savings through a partnership with local utilities. Through twice yearly service calls, we will deliver the best value and greatest security for our clients. We are focused on customer service that is well communicated, rapid in execution and responsive to the needs of our customers."

Next, provide a brief overview of the target markets that you identified while working with your team through Chapter 3 of this book. Remind the reader of what your focus areas should be based on market potential and who you will be targeting in your marketing efforts. In the same chapter you reviewed and evaluated your competition so it's a good idea to also include some brief information about how your messaging to the market will position you to beat the competition.

In Chapter 4, your team worked through the company goals. You'll want to include them in your executive summary as those are the numbers that you are trying to help reach through your marketing efforts.

Brand initiatives were covered next. The summary should just touch on key activities. For instance, from the summary you would want them to take away that branding efforts will be increased with more education and engagement from your employees. If they want to know more about what specific engagements will take place, they can seek it out in the plan to gain a more in-depth understanding.

If new tools and technologies are part of the plan, be sure to mention it but don't go into detail. The executive summary is not about the tactical. Keep it high level and relatively short, not more than one to two pages in length. It is the summary of all your work.

Action items

1. As a leadership team review the plan and pull out the key elements of goals, purpose, mission and branding.

2. Create an executive summary that is then reviewed by the leadership team.

Notes

CHAPTER 11

Implementing & Communicating Your Marketing Plan

Now that you have developed your marketing plan and know what you want to do, it's time to figure out how to implement it. If you don't have the budget to hire a marketing person, you'll need to take a look at what resources you may already have in place inside your company.

Start by making a list of the employees that you currently have who aren't working in the field. What is their work background? Did they attend college? What was their field of study? It's possible that you might have a hidden gem in your office that can take on some of the tasks involved in your marketing plans.

If, after performing this analysis of your current team, you don't think anyone would be able to handle the implementation, consider contracting with an outside consultant who knows the roofing industry. They will evaluate the plan (maybe even help you improve upon it) and determine a set number of hours each month to manage your marketing plan and activities.

The advantage to this approach is that you will get an experienced marketing professional for less than the cost of a full-time employee. The consultant will have contacts with designers, web developers, SEO experts and writers which will ensure that your ads, brochures, website, etc. are professional and within your brand guidelines.

It's important to remember as you implement your marketing plan, that it is just a plan. And it's ok for plans to change as you go. As you monitor campaigns and track results it might become necessary to make a change. Not every ad or email will work. The message might need to be changed.

It's also important to remember that it takes time to build momentum. You won't always see immediate results. In fact, studies show that someone needs to see or hear a message seven times before they remember it. Determine what your key performance indicators (KPIs) will be for each part of your campaign. Your KPIs could be the number of people who complete a form on your website, the number of people who download a piece of content or view a video, or the number of interactions you have on social media each week. Determining these before you get started will help you evaluate what is working and what might need to be adjusted.

Next, it's time to share the plans with the rest of the company. This is a critical step in a successful plan that many companies overlook.

By sharing your plan with your employees, you can create excitement, generate buy-in and ensure that everyone is aware of what you will be doing to generate leads and market the business. There is nothing more embarrassing than having a potential customer call in and mention an offer that they either saw in an ad or received in the mail and your employee who answered the phone doesn't know what the caller is talking about.

You don't need to bury your team in the finer details of the marketing plan, but they need to understand that you are going to begin focused, targeted marketing activities and you want them on board and excited about it.

Tell them the why behind your efforts. Perhaps you are embarking on a marketing campaign that will position your company as the leak repair expert in your service area. In that case, you would want your employees to understand that goal. They would be empowered to share that message throughout their customer interactions and in their conversations outside of work with friends and families which reinforces your marketing effort.

Take the bigger picture parts of your marketing plan and put together a PowerPoint deck that you can share at a company meeting or lunch and learn event. Be sure to explain why you prepared a marketing plan and share your goals with the team. Use the remaining slides to provide an overview of the kinds of activities you plan to undertake and the promotions or special offers that you are considering how they can be a part of the plan's success.

Your internal communication is going to be key in keeping your employees on the same page with your marketing efforts. Every time a new initiative, advertisement, email campaign, postcard, print ad etc. is about to go into effect it is critical to send a copy of it out to your team before it goes live. Let them know during the presentation that they don't have to remember everything you are telling them today because you will be communicating with them throughout the year as each of your initiatives goes into play.

End by asking for feedback and questions. Your employees interact with customers and potential customers every day. They may have a fresh perspective or an insight to offer that you and your team who developed the plan might never have considered.

Action items
1. Evaluate the members of your team to assess if anyone has the skill set to help implement the marketing plan.

2. Secure the services of an industry-experienced marketing expert to assess and implement activities.

3. Schedule an employee event, lunch and learn or breakfast to kick off the plan. If freshening your brand or logo is part of the plan, consider doing that before the presentation and providing a promo item or clothing with the updated logo as part of the presentation.

4. Put together the slides to communicate the larger parts of the plan to your team.

Notes

Appendix 1 – Marketing Plan Structure

1. **Executive Summary**
2. **Company Positioning Statement**
    a. Mission Statement
    b. Services
    c. Commitment
    d. Value Proposition
3. **Markets**
    a. High End Residential
    b. Light Commercial
    c. Solar
4. **Yearly Goals**
    a. Company
    b. Divisions / Departments
    c. Community
    d. Special Messaging / Initiatives
5. **Branding**
    a. Brand Promise
    b. Logo Updates
    c. Branding Guide
    d. Brand Ambassadors
6. **Marketing Tools**
    a. Overall Branding and Look Review
    b. Website Review
    c. Video
    d. Content Marketing
    e. Advertising
    f. Marketing Automation
    g. Public Relations
    h. Tradeshows
    i. Association Involvement
7. **Technology Considerations**
8. **Marketing automation**
    a. CRM
    b. Email marketing
    c. Smart devices
    d. Customer portals
    e. Website

Appendix 2 – Target Markets

Service to promote	Target market	Where do I reach them?
Commercial roof maintenance	Facility managers; commercial real estate managers	Online (sharing articles on your company blog and paid advertising), Twitter, professional associations, LinkedIn, LinkedIn groups
Commercial roof restoration/coatings	Facility managers, building owners	Online (sharing articles on your company blog and paid advertising), Twitter, professional associations, LinkedIn, LinkedIn groups
Commercial roof replacement	Facility managers, building owners	Online (sharing articles on your company blog and paid advertising), Twitter, professional associations, LinkedIn, LinkedIn groups
Commercial new construction	Architect, engineers and general contractors	Professional associations, LinkedIn, LinkedIn groups
Residential asphalt shingle re-roofs	Homeowners with roofs aged 20+ years	Online (SEO, blogs, Google AdWords), on Facebook, email, home shows
Residential storm damage	Homeowners	Online (SEO, blogs, Google AdWords); on Facebook; email; targeting geographic post storm
Specialty residential roofs	Homeowners with home value of $300,000 or higher	Online (SEO, blogs, AdWords), on Facebook, email, home shows

Appendix 3 – Sample Marketing Planner

	Jan	Feb	Mar
Brand	Updates as needed; Begin using tagline	Maintain	Launch new system options
Collateral	Develop materials	Finish and print materials, begin using	Determine if any additional materials needed
Website	Meeting with web vendor	Website facelift finishes and launches by month end	Ongoing content on blog and SEO optimization
PR/Social/Blog ideas	New hires PR	Hail damage article	New, enhanced website and announce referral program
Promotions	Order promo items and shirts	Hand out branded shirts to crew	Roof inspection discount
Print Ads	Design 1/4 pg ad	Begin 1/4 pg ad	Continue ads
Digital Ads	Design	Begin targeted digital advertising	Continue targeted online ads

Appendix 4 - Marketing Budget Template

Budget Code	Jan	Feb	Mar	Apr	May	Jun	Jul	Aug	Sep	Oct	Nov	Dec	Total
Website													
Advertising													
Tradeshows / Events													
Printing & Outside Services													
Promotional Items													
Dues													
Opportunity Fund													
Total													

Conclusion

We would like to thank you for taking the time to read and use this workbook to develop your marketing plan. Plans are only as good as the people and the passion that help create them. Writing this book is a passion for both of us. Creating tools that are specific to the roofing industry is important and part of our commitment to the roofing industry.

We would like to thank our families and friends who encourage us and take the time to help us proof and edit this book. Your feedback and insights are much appreciated.

Thank you to RoofersCoffeeShop.com and National Roofing Contractors Association for helping us to distribute this series of publications.

Good luck with your upcoming marketing plan. It can make all the difference for your business, your employees and your success.

Thank you!

Heidi and Karen

Heidi J. Ellsworth
hje@ellsworth.us

Karen L. Edwards
karen@casimirgroupllc.com

www.ingramcontent.com/pod-product-compliance
Lightning Source LLC
Chambersburg PA
CBHW050233230526
45470CB00005B/1935